Kids Can Help
FIGHT POVERTY

by Emily Raij

Consultant: Lisa Joyslin, Inclusive Volunteerism Program
Manager, Minnesota Association for Volunteer Administration,
St. Paul, Minnesota

CAPSTONE PRESS
a capstone imprint

Capstone Captivate is published by Capstone Press, an imprint of Capstone.
1710 Roe Crest Drive
North Mankato, Minnesota 56003
www.capstonepub.com

Library of Congress Cataloging-in-Publication Data is available on the Library of Congress website.
ISBN 978-1-4966-8378-6 (library binding)
ISBN 978-1-4966-8784-5 (paperback)
ISBN 978-1-4966-8429-5 (ebook pdf)

Summary: Make the world a better place for people in need! This book is full of ideas and projects readers can put into action to fight poverty.

Image Credits
Getty Images: Orange County Register/Digital First Media/Leonard Ortiz, 14, WireImage/Paul Zimmerman, 17; iStockphoto: adamkaz, 22, FatCamera, 29, fstop123, cover, 19, kali9, 26, SDI Productions, back cover, 8, 27, Weekend Images Inc., 25; Newscom: Zuma Press/John Westberg, 13, Zuma Press/Modesto Bee, 15; Pixabay: DavidZydd (stripe background), 1 and throughout; Shutterstock: Africa Studio, 4, alla puhacheva, 23 (bottom), Andy Dean Photography, 7, Aspects and Angles, 11, HASPhotos, 9, humphery, 24, Jen Wolf, 16, Mark stock, 21 (bottom), michelmond, 23 (top), Monkey Business Images, 5, 28, Pormezz, 6, Sabira Dewji, 20, 21 (top), Sorbis, 10, SpeedKingz, 12

Editorial Credits
Editor: Erika L. Shores; Designers: Sara Radka and Elyse White; Media Researcher: Svetlana Zhurkin; Production Specialist: Tori Abraham

All internet sites appearing in back matter were available and accurate when this book was sent to press.

Words in **bold** are in the glossary.

Printed in the United States of America.
PA117

TABLE OF CONTENTS

Hunger and Homelessness

What makes your home a nice place to live? Is it your soft bed? Do you enjoy your favorite meals at home? Maybe you have neighbors you play with after school. Everyone needs food and a place to live. A warm home and good food keep us safe, healthy, and happy.

» Every person needs a safe place to live.

» Having enough food to eat is a basic human need.

It can be hard for people to get what they need sometimes. Hunger means not getting enough food to eat each day. It can also mean not getting enough **nutritious** food. Sometimes people don't have grocery stores with fresh food where they live. People also may not have the money to buy enough food.

» People pay bills so they have water, electricity, and internet in their homes.

Having a home costs a great deal of money. There are many bills to pay, such as rent and electricity. Sometimes people can't pay their bills. There are many reasons this can happen. People might get sick. Then they have to pay doctor bills. Paying for medical care may mean people don't have enough to pay other bills.

If adults are sick, they also can't work. Without jobs, people can't pay for things they need. They may lose their homes and become **homeless**. It's hard for adults to work when they are hungry or don't have a place to sleep at night. When kids are hungry or tired, it's hard to learn at school.

» A homeowner who cannot work may need to sell his or her house.

What Can I Do?

Do you care about fighting **poverty**? You can help **charities** that give food and **shelter** to people. Charities are groups that take care of people's most important needs. Food banks and soup kitchens give people food. Homeless shelters offer a safe place to live for a short time. These groups may collect money to help people. You can help them raise money.

» Soup kitchens are places where people in need can eat meals.

» A volunteer uses a list to help sort food at a town food bank.

You can also **volunteer** directly at places. Food banks might need help stocking shelves and passing out food. Shelters may need help collecting blankets and other supplies. Think about ways you like to help. Do you like planning events? You can come up with creative ways to raise money. Use what you like doing to help others.

Helping those in need shows you care about more than just yourself. You are being a good person in the world. All people should have their basic needs met and feel safe. There can be unfair reasons why people's needs aren't being met. For example, some **policies** make it hard for families without much money to find affordable places to live. Those families may not have stores close by that sell healthy food.

» Small convenience stores might be the closest places for some people to shop for food. The food at these stores often is not very healthy.

» Activists come together to hold signs in order to raise awareness about people who are living in poverty.

Activists take steps to make things fair. They want **justice,** or fair answers to unfair policies or laws. They talk to lawmakers and officials to change policies that are unfair or hurt people.

Service Projects

Food banks or pantries give free food to people who don't have enough. These places need donations of food and money. You can raise money for a local food bank or pantry. Hold a student and teacher talent show at your school and sell tickets. Performers can sing, dance, read poems, tell stories, and more.

A talent show gives people the chance to show off their skills. It is also fun and can be a good fundraiser. Work with adults at your school and parents to make a schedule for the show. You can sell tickets before or after school. Ask teachers if you can send flyers about the show home with students. Make posters about the event to hang up at school.

» Putting together a school talent show can raise money for local food banks.

Items Food Pantries Need

- applesauce
- canned vegetables
- shelf-stable or powdered milk
- meals in a box/meal kits
- herbs and spices
- canned or dried fruit
- granola bars
- instant mashed potatoes
- crackers
- cooking oil
- canned chicken, tuna, salmon, and other meat
- peanut butter
- rice
- nuts
- healthy cereal
- canned beans, soup, stew, and chili
- toilet paper
- pasta

The Empty Bowl Project

Fourth-grade students in Bastrop, Texas, painted bowls in art class. The bowls were sold at a dinner to raise money for a local food pantry. The fundraiser is called the Empty Bowl Project and raises **awareness** of hunger. Each student painted two or more bowls. To go with the bowls, local chefs made a dinner of soups, stews, and chili. People in the community buy tickets to the annual dinner and can also buy the students' bowls to raise even more money.

» A shoe drive is a service project students everywhere can do.

Raising money is one way to help charities. Collecting goods is another. People often have things they can donate. And they are happy to give to a good cause. For example, you can hold a shoe drive at school. Collect gently used or new shoes. You may need to ask for donations of bins or large boxes to store the shoes. Make posters to let people know about the shoe drive. Hang them up at school. Be sure to explain that shoes must be clean and in good, wearable condition or new.

Your drive can help people near or far. You can work with a local group that gives shoes to people in your community. Or you can collect for a larger charity like Soles4Souls. They help get shoes to people in all 50 states and more than 100 countries.

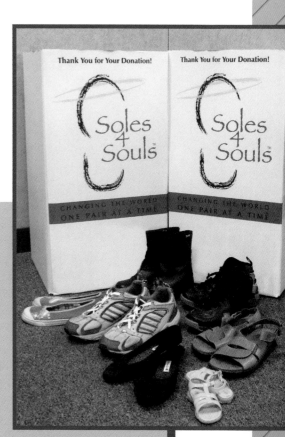

Shoes for Everyone

Ten-year-old Traci Weinstein from New York worked with Soles4Souls to collect shoes for those in need. She learned that not having shoes kept children from attending school and adults from going to work all over the world. Traci was born in Guatemala. She chose to collect shoes for people there because of the high-poverty level. In just a few months, Traci collected more than 30,000 pairs of shoes in her community! She beat her goal of 25,000 pairs and made a big difference.

» People can donate tomatoes from the plants they grow to local food banks.

Do you like to garden? Use your green thumb to feed people in your town or neighborhood. You can plant a garden and give away the food you grow. Not only do some people not get enough to eat, but they don't get enough fresh fruits and vegetables. This is especially true in high-poverty areas. If you have room in your yard or even on your windowsill, you can grow food. Then you can donate some or all of it to a local soup kitchen. Your gift of fresh food will help with hunger and health.

Katie's Krops

When Katie Stagliano of Summerville, South Carolina, was 9 years old, she brought home a cabbage seedling from school and planted it. But she never expected it would grow to 40 pounds (18 kilograms)! She wanted to do something special with the giant vegetable, so she gave it to a local soup kitchen. Helping to feed people inspired Katie to start Katie's Krops. Katie's Krops is a group that plants gardens to grow food for soup kitchens. Now there are more than 100 Katie's Krops gardens across the United States. They are all run by kids between 9 and 16 years old.

Collecting and donating food are important steps to fighting hunger. But food banks often need help packing up and bringing the food to people too. Not everyone has a way to get to the food banks. Food banks may not have enough workers to deliver the food. Seniors and people with disabilities may not be able to drive. They especially need help getting food.

You can help pack up meals and supplies and get them to people in need. Ask a parent or other adult to drive you and a friend to deliver food. You could also work to set up volunteer drivers through your clubs or other activities. It's important to bring meals and smiles to those who have trouble leaving their homes to get food.

» Some people are not able to leave their homes to get food. It is important to help bring food donations to them.

Would you like to have a party with a purpose? Make snack and personal care bags to give to homeless shelters. You can host a party where you ask friends to bring items for the bags. Or you can ask friends to bring these items instead of birthday gifts. Then pack the bags together.

» Putting together bags of basic items makes it easy for shelter workers to give them to people in need.

» Basic items can help people experiencing homelessness.

Snack bags should include food that will stay fresh for a while. Crackers, nuts, water, applesauce cups, and granola bars are good choices. Personal care bags can have small sizes of toothpaste, a toothbrush, floss, soap, sunscreen, and hand sanitizer. You can also include combs, cleaning wipes, socks, and bandages or other first aid items.

 HELPING FACT

Some hotels take part in a soap recycling program through Clean the World. Used soap is melted down and made into new bars. Clean the World has sent more than 53 million bars to more than 127 countries. Staying clean prevents disease and even death.

» Find out why people become homeless and then share what you find out with others.

If people learn more about poverty, they can help more. You can spread awareness. Do some **research**. Then put together a list of facts about how and why people become homeless. Try to make your fact sheet local. Include information about homelessness in your area. Ask to post your fact sheet on message boards at libraries, cafés, and gyms.

For example, many people become homeless due to unlucky events. They might lose a job, have an accident, or become ill. Others go through a natural disaster. This makes it hard to earn money. Then people can't pay for their homes. Other people work but do not earn enough to pay all their bills every month. They may have to choose between paying for food or doctor bills.

Immigrants or **refugees** who are new to this country can experience poverty. They may be starting with very little as they try to build a new life. They might not have enough money for a house or apartment. They may have difficulty finding jobs if they are still learning English. These families might need help from charities and community members as they start out in a new country.

» If strong storms cause a great deal of flooding, it sometimes forces people to leave their homes.

HELPING FACT

Natural disasters, such as floods, storms, and earthquakes, cause about 14 million people to become homeless each year.

What If I Want to Do More?

Everyone deserves to have enough food to eat and a safe place to live. It doesn't seem fair that some people are hungry or homeless. Some housing policies are unfair too. They might say people have to earn a certain amount of money to live in a place. That makes it hard for people who do not have a lot of money to find homes. Some poorer areas may not have many stores that sell fresh fruits and vegetables. That keeps people from getting healthy food.

» A company might tear down an apartment building and put up a new building with rents people can no longer afford.

» You can write letters to people in charge and ask them to think about people living in poverty.

Policies may not be fair. But they can be changed. This is where activists help. What if a building company wants to tear down low-cost housing and build expensive apartments? Many people won't be able to afford the high-priced apartments. An activist can **protest** this. Activism can be quiet or behind the scenes. You can write letters to lawmakers or your local newspaper. Post your ideas on social media with a parent's OK. Pass out information at town hall meetings or community events.

Caring for Everyone

Food and shelter are things everyone needs. And everyone deserves to have their basic needs met. You can help fight poverty. There are always people in your community who need help. You just have to find what you like to do and where you can do it. Whether you want to collect food or grow it, there is a project for you. Find one that makes good use of your time and talent. Think about how you like to help. You can help on your own or with a group. Start a school project or work with your family. Hunger and homelessness are big problems. No act of help is too small.

» You can grow vegetables to give away to food banks.

» You can use some of your free time to help collect food for people in your community.

Other Ways to Get Involved

» Bring in extra class snacks for your teacher to put in a bin so that students who are unable or forget to bring in snacks do not go hungry.

» Visit local restaurants and grocery stores to see if they can donate the food they can't sell, such as leftovers or dented cans, to shelters and pantries. Check with the pantries first to make sure they take these items.

» Set up a Little Free Pantry in your neighborhood. Be sure to check local laws before you set one up. At these pantries, people can give and take food as needed from a small box set up in a park or other public area.

» Put together a school supply drive before the school year begins. Give the supplies to food banks or homeless shelters that are collecting items for students whose families cannot afford pencils, paper, glue, and other things.

» Start a Students Against Hunger club to let people know about world hunger. Make posters with facts about hunger and poverty in other countries. Hang the posters around school.

» Tell lawmakers your thoughts about programs that feed hungry kids. Write or call your governor and leaders in Congress to discuss food programs that help children and families.

» Have a winter coat and used clothing drive at your school. Ask others to help you sort, hang up, and display the clothes. Then, families in need from your school can choose items privately. Remaining items can be given to shelters or other charities.

Glossary

activist (AC-tiv-ist)—a person who works for social or political change

awareness (uh-WIHR-ness)—knowledge or concern about a situation

charity (CHAYR-uh-tee)—a group that raises money or collects goods to help people in need

homeless (HOHM-less)—to not have a regular or stable place to live

immigrant (IM-uh-gruhnt)—a person who leaves one country and settles in another

justice (JUHSS-tiss)—fair action or treatment

nutritious (noo-TRISH-uhss)—containing the vitamins and minerals the body uses to stay strong and healthy

policy (POL-uh-see)—a general plan that people use to help them make decisions or take action

poverty (PAW-vuhr-tee)—the condition of lacking money and belongings

protest (pro-TEST)—to speak out about something strongly and publicly

refugee (ref-yuh-JEE)—a person who has to leave a place to escape a disaster or war

research (REE-surch)—the collecting of information about a subject

shelter (SHEL-tur)—a safe place where people can stay

volunteer (vol-uhn-TIHR)—to offer to do something without pay

Read More

Clinton, Chelsea. *Start Now! You Can Make a Difference.* New York: Penguin Random House, 2018.

Roberts, Jillian and Jaime Casap. *On Our Street: Our First Talk about Poverty.* Custer, WA: Orca Book Publishers, 2018.

Spilsbury, Louise. *Poverty and Hunger.* London: Hachette Children's Books, 2017.

Internet Sites

Be a Volunteer
kidshealth.org/en/kids/volunteering.html

Kids Can Make a Difference: Hunger Facts
kidscanmakeadifference.org/hunger-facts

Index